Absolutely Typical Too

The Art Dealer

Absolutely Typical Too

words by Victoria Mather
pictures by
Sue Macartney-Snape

with a foreword by Richard Ingrams

MORE OF THE BEST OF

SOCIAL STEREOTYPES

FROM THE

Telegraph Magazine

Methuen

First published in Great Britain in 1997
by Methuen London

1 3 5 7 9 10 8 6 4 2

This paperback edition published in 1998 by Methuen
an imprint of Random House UK Ltd
20 Vauxhall Bridge Road, London SW1V 2SA

Random House Australia (Pty) Limited
20 Alfred Street, Milsons Point, Sydney,
New South Wales 2061, Australia

Random House New Zealand Limited
18 Poland Road, Glenfield,
Auckland 10, New Zealand

Random House South Africa (Pty) Limited
Endulini, 5A Jubilee Road, Parktown 2193, South Africa

Random House UK Limited Reg. No. 954009

All the Social Stereotypes in this volume
were originally published in 1995, 1996 and 1997
in the *Telegraph Magazine*

ISBN 0 413 71790 9 (hardback)
ISBN 0 413 72100 0 (paperback)
A CIP catalogue record for this book
is available at the British Library

Typeset by MATS, Southend-on-Sea, Essex
Printed and bound in Singapore
by Tien Wah Press

Foreword

In the heady days of the sixties when *Private Eye* was getting into its stride and we had a Labour Prime Minister at Number Ten, some of us assumed (naïvely, as it turned out) that great social changes were afoot. The rich, the upper classes could expect, if not tumbrils, then an end to some of their perks and privileges. The monarchy was doomed, public schools would almost certainly go, the House of Lords was for the scrap heap. In the new era of equality, magazines like *Tatler* and *Harpers*, which catered to the worst kind of snobbish instincts, were bound to fade away.

In the event, of course, nothing of the kind happened. When the smoke cleared all the old pieces were still on the board – guards officers, debutantes, the lot. Society (meaning High Society) continued to behave as if the nice, gentlemanly Sir Alec Douglas-Home was still running the show. Jennifer went on writing her diary and the same horsey faces under the same improbable hats smiled inanely at weddings, charity auctions and point-to-points.

Many years later when Mr Major proclaimed the arrival of a classless society, he was greeted with a hollow laugh by anyone of a certain age. His reign, after all, had coincided with the extraordinary success of the film *Four Weddings and a Funeral* which celebrated the lifestyle of a group of feckless Sloane Rangers all portrayed with great affection and never a hint of satire.

All the more reason to welcome another collection of social stereotypes from that dastardly duo Victoria Mather and Sue Macartney-Snape. You can tell from the accuracy of observation in the words and the drawings that these two are insiders. But there is not a trace of nostalgia or snobby fellow feeling in these portraits. Victoria Mather may move in all the right kind of circles but she remains a brilliant journalist, alert to every little social nuance. At her best Sue Macartney-Snape recalls the mad savagery of the early Ronald Searle who classified so many of these British prototypes at an earlier stage in their development. Even the Old-fashioned

Nanny fiercely clutching her medicine bottle is a forbidding figure who terrorises the children in her care. Having myself suffered the indignity of taking a family heirloom for valuation at Sotheby's only to be told that it was a worthless fake, I warm especially to the Auction House Expert, complete with striped shirt and over-long hair, peering with fishlike eyes at a hideous oriental vase.

We feel we know these characters only too well and much of the fun will be to try and guess the identity of the real people who have inspired their creators. I do not live near enough to the heart of Chelsea to score a great many points in any such game. But the sapphic Lady Novelist who lives in North London and cuts her own hair seems more than a little familiar. And that History Don called Norman who goes on telly all the time and conducts his tutorials in the pub – wasn't there someone rather like that in the papers only the other day?

Nuff said. I know I shall have this little book in my loo for many years to come. Some people may think that insulting, but I couldn't pay the authors a higher compliment. *Absolutely Typical Too* will form part of a very select library – *The British Character* by 'Pont', Osbert Lancaster's *Pocket Cartoons*, *The Sloane Ranger's Handbook* – not to mention some yellowing, dog-eared copies of *Private Eye*.

Richard Ingrams
April 1997

To our godchildren

To Scarlett Lacey, Meg Guy, Alexander Turner, Charles Sanders, Tom Butterfield, Anna Mitchell, Rachel Wrey, Tilly Leon, Louis Levi and Sophie Coleridge, with all my love, Godmother Victoria

and

to Alexander Littler, Alexander Wallace, Annabel Farrant, Hamish Robinson, Isabella Adams, and Johnny, Milo and Poppy Royds, with love, Sue

The heroine of this book is Emma Soames, editor of the *Daily Telegraph* Magazine, who fearlessly continues to publish Social Stereotypes despite the magazine, writer and illustrator operating in three different continents, respectively Canary Wharf, London and New York. She is not only a long distance comfort blanket but unfailingly laughs at our jokes. Warm thanks again to Sarah Miller, who marriage-broked our original partnership and Mary Chamberlain, who once more has edited the cast of characters to whom many unique, entirely non-stereotypical people have contributed invaluable insider information.

The Harassed Mother

The dog's eaten the pork stuffing, the fairy lights have fused and at least one child has been sick. In short, Christmas has caught the young mother in the small of the back with all the force of the down express. The tree is blighted by wonky, twisted ornaments made by her three children at nursery school. Her husband has driven to Devon to fetch his mother, a wet sock of a woman whose idea of festivity is a timid sherry and a mince pie. A vile smell of burning indicates that she is going to be disappointed about the mince pies and Belinda takes to the bottle with the careless rapture of the hysterical. So this is Christmas-in-our-own-home-darling so rosily envisaged when they moved to Oxfordshire: perpetual rain and permanent darkness. In London the dark afternoons were illuminated by blissful shop windows and the coal-effect fire never necessitated soggy trips to the woodshed. On her second glass Belinda remembers that she's forgotten to peel the chestnuts or make the brandy butter, but has ceased to care. Four-year-old Joshua meanwhile sellotapes Louise to a table leg. It is at this point that the gumboil of a mother-in-law arrives in pained tut-tut mode, noting the bottle – 'Celebrating already, are we, dear?' – and then martyring herself by making little crosses in the untended Brussels sprouts. Belinda arrives at midnight mass with ragged tinsel still in her hair – Minnie's attempt to turn Mummy into a fairy – stays up until three in the morning wrapping presents and has to wake at six to put the turkey in the oven. Opening their stockings, the children wonder why Father Christmas has left the price on everything.

The Butcher

Old Rectory telephones unto Old Rectory in frenzied excitement about Mr Robinson's new line in sausages: 'Caroline? I popped into Robinson's this morning to get Edward's beastly pheasants plucked and he's making these marvellous chestnut chipolatas for Christmas.' There is a reverent silence as each contemplates Mr Robinson's rubicund versatility. The country butcher, with his splendid slabs of dark brown, well hung beef, is a beacon shining through the sterile uniformity of supermarket shopping. By calling Caroline 'Madam', and allowing her to run an account, Mr Robinson conforms to her idea of a life-support system to the gentry. They have cosy chats about the iniquity of EC regulations while he is chopping the feet off chickens and she takes all her London friends there when they come to stay for the weekend; a visit to Robinson's has quite replaced antiqueing on Saturday mornings. Whole beef fillets are carted home to the freezers of Fulham. Mr Robinson, while jovial in receipt of this patronage, is well aware that it is his mince and chicken customers who keep him in business; that and diversification. There isn't much call for scrag end nowadays, but he's had great success with a line in home-made veal and ham pies, fresh pasta and his spicy tomato sauce. The latter is a counter-attack against the vegetarian tendency, since they've had any amount of trouble with the BSE scares. It's the young – they believe anything they see on the telly – but get their parents into the shop for a bit of pasta and Mr Robinson is confident he can sell Mum a nice leg of lamb. He's also very obliging about vacuum-packing the boy scouts' clothes for their adventure camp in the Brecon Beacons. Really, where would the village be without him?

The Stepmother

Nancy feels more traumatised than if she had broken a nail – her stepchildren are coming for Christmas. She married for love but not for turkey, plum pudding and the appalling sight of her teenage stepdaughter's pierced navel. Domesticity does not loom large in the world of multimedia publishing and for some years Christmas has meant a bronze-up in the Caribbean. Being American she celebrates Thanksgiving, but with dear friends in Connecticut who have battalions of white-gloved, soft-footed minions. She now fears that something more festive than a Christmas tree decorated by an interior designer is expected. Stephen, whose only fault as a husband is his children, is sublimely oblivious to the inconvenience to which she is being put. 'Darling, it's wonderful that Tania and Jeremy want to come to us. You can take Tania shopping – I know she'd like that – and I really need to talk to Jeremy, I think he aspires to be Nick Leeson.' Nancy would rather be seen without make-up than with Tania in Bergdorf's. Tania would rather be in TriBeCa. Friends did warn Nancy that marrying a Brit working in New York might be a fashion statement but remember the heavy baggage: a country Camilla of a first wife in England, Stephen's fabulous success as a Wall Street banker draining away into her equine pursuits, the children insatiable for keys to his exquisite Cheyne Walk house. Nancy thought the Atlantic was between her and all that. She realised her mistake when Tania first came to stay and said brightly, 'Hello, Nancy, Mummy says you've had a face-lift.'

The Animal Breeder

When she was a debutante Lady Clarissa used her clothes allowance to buy her first cow. It was a black Dexter, three and a half foot high and the bovine equivalent of the Thelwell pony. Her father, a Friesian man himself, told her she was a chump but Lady Clarissa's devotion to Dexters has remained stalwart throughout two marriages and a colourful widowhood on the circuit of the better agricultural shows. She is the Dexter expert, having an even more arcane knowledge than that of the duchesses who so ardently champion Jacob sheep. Letters to her children at school used to read: 'Moonbeam cast her calf. Very troublesome.' A youthful sojourn in Kenya with her first husband proved sadly unproductive in terms of cattle breeding (the heat, the flies, the lions) and, in truth, she was quite relieved when he died and she could return to the embracing environs of Yorkshire, sell her diamonds and buy a champion bull. Her second husband was a mild-mannered literary critic whose bohemian friends thought the cows perfectly sweet, a happy confluence of aestheticism and agriculture. Weekends at Lady Clarissa's are renowned for the splendid company, excellent malt whisky and amusing disregard for any other form of human comfort since she is interested only in the outdoors. The literary critic finally expired of pneumonia but Lady Clarissa has, only this winter, installed under-floor heating in the cattle shed.

The Ski Instructor

Jean-Yves is a suave streak of Gallic fascination. Many a Charlotte and Lucinda has returned to Gloucestershire with her heart beating a little faster beneath her Barbour at the memory of Jean-Yves's incredible cool down the *couloirs*. Bronzed, frighteningly fit and with a personality considerably enhanced by his jazzy ski monitor's uniform, he makes their banker husbands look quite porcine. They book him for the next season and he arrives at Chalet Christophe on the first evening to drink all their duty-free while planning the week's skiing. This is selectively angled towards bibulous lunches at his brother's, cousin's and uncle's mountain restaurants where *le patron* appears at the critical moment after vast amounts of burgundy have been consumed, generously proffering glasses of the local *digestif* from hideously shaped bottles. It is only afterwards that the bankers realise they have been charged for this privilege, but write it off to the euphoria of Jean-Yves's charm. What the hell. Jean-Yves is such a sweetie. 'Follow in my tracks!' he cries and so they do, like lambs, through thick crust and white-outs. 'Bend zee knees!' is his other exhortation and this year he will have them all on parabolic skis (hired from his father's shop) carving their turns. In summer this demigod sustains his perma-tan as a windsurfing instructor in the South of France.

The Cruft's Dog Breeder

The Lower Mongolian Swamp Hound, to which Christine has devoted her middle age, is a breed only recently allowed by the Kennel Club. To the benevolent eye, Champion Tirakau Aurora of Penge (known as Dotty at home) is a creature of sublime beauty, tail waving like a flag. To the ignorant she appears to be a hirsute mobile brick. Christine's put-upon husband, Bert, thankfully waved them off to the NEC in a battered Ford estate car upholstered in dog hair and with a sticker in the rear window proclaiming 'Show Dogs in Transit'. He is denied the great treat of Cruft's by the necessity of tending the latest litter of little swamp hounds; Christine and Dotty, staying with a long-lost aunt hastily rediscovered in the environs of Birmingham, are immersed in the bacchanalia of dogdom. Mongolian Swamp Hound umbrellas are on sale for the first time this year, not to mention dangly hound earrings and toy breed cigarette cards. In between blow-drying Dotty and tending her with Carmen rollers, Christine has bought Bert a commemorative tea towel and consumed a vast amount of sandwiches from squashed foil packets. Dotty technically only eats dried Woofit (Christine dreams of the commercials consequent upon a Best of Breed win) but is indulged in an unofficial penchant for chicken. Confined with other owners amongst a plethora of cages with irascible, overbred inhabitants, the Cruft's dog breeder becomes decidedly bitchy. Her peers are universally deficient in correct dietary, reproductive or grooming etiquette. Legs are too long, hair is too short, eyes are too dull, nose too pointed, conformation too unorthodox. When Christine returns with this heartening litany of ills, Bert is uncertain whether she is talking about the dogs or their owners.

The Honeymoon Couple

Rory insisted that the honeymoon remained a secret. 'Darling, you'll hardly need to pack a thing, we'll be all alone, far away from anyone,' he'd said. Georgie, swooning with romance, thought that since it was March he must mean Mauritius. Scotland never, ever crossed her mind. They are indeed alone: Glen Oykle is nearer the mountains of the moon than the local village. Apart from the sepulchral Mrs McTavish, who leaves a succession of Pyrex dishes containing brown food on the spluttering kitchen range, they have seen no one for a week. The shooting lodge has twenty bedrooms, none with a double bed, and the fire smokes; Georgie, nurtured in the centrally heated Home Counties, has worn a borrowed coat at all times, including breakfast. She has also cried a lot, demented with exhaustion after the wedding and the hideous memory of the best man's speech. The telephone doesn't work, so she cannot ring her mother, and Rory's idea of comfort and solace is bracing walks, revisiting the murky pools on the River Oyk where he used to fish as a boy. 'This is my favourite place in all the world, darling,' he murmurs. 'I knew you'd love it here too.' Georgie is unable to envisage those sunlit, boyhood days as she watches the vertical curtain of rain progressing up the glen. Can this be the suave commodity broker with whom she fell in love? In a panic induced by the severing of her umbilical cord with Harvey Nichols, she wonders if she will ever again wear a piece of clothing that doesn't smell of wet dog. When she clings to Rory for warmth, he interprets it as being wondrously feminine. When he gets a horrid cold, Georgie realises something her mother never told her: being a wife is also being a nurse.

The Bed and Breakfast Landlady

Mrs Philpotts is all of a dither. The Fire Brigade is about to carry out their annual inspection of her exits and although Mr P has ungummed the door on the landing with a chisel and WD40, one can never be too sure. Mrs Philpotts has had a little nip to calm her poor nerves, so when the inspectors do arrive they are greeted with a smiling blast of Harvey's Bristol Cream heavily overlaid with Colgate. Indeed, number 45 Verdun Road ('You can't miss us, dear, we're next to the Cuddly Cod fish and chip shop') is a symphony of contrasting aromas. There's the hearty base of fry-up: years of sausage, baked beans, tinned tomatoes, fried eggs, fried bread, mushrooms and that sort of bacon which oozes strange white scum. Mrs Philpotts prides herself on her breakfast, souvenirs of which are embedded in her swirly sunburst yellow carpet. The oily charms of Cuddly Cod seep through the bobbly wallpaper, but her counter-offensive is a fog of Silk Cut and a series of Forest Glade air freshening tablets in pink plastic holders. The lavatory paper is Camay pink, also the frilly lampshades in bedrooms overwhelmed by matching floral curtains, sheets and duvet covers. Mrs Philpotts likes a bit of colour, and was the first in the road to have an avocado bathroom suite. 'You spoil us, Mrs P,' her regulars say as they stand in the particularly dark part of the corridor where she's installed a pay-phone. What no one has worked out is why, since number 45 is only bed and breakfast, it always smells predominantly of cabbage.

The Auction House Expert

Nicholas Fotherington has perfected the brand of unctuous charm so essential for ingratiating himself with widows in possession of old masters. He reads the obituaries avidly each morning, hoping that the deceased will have left strict instructions that all their things are to be sold through nice Mr Fotherington at Christoby's. But such windfalls are infrequent in these days of vulgar commerce; sometimes he thinks, with a fastidious shudder, that it is only his Hilditch & Key shirt which distinguishes him from the auctioneers of cattle in obscure little country towns. The young Fothers, like so many hopeful second sons of the gentry, started at Christoby's as a porter, an initiation period of handling the *objets* with reverence and taste. Judged to have 'the eye', he became a junior expert; then his future seemed so gracious, only full of pleasant surprises like happening upon a Wemyss pig. Now the enchanted world of impressionable American collectors and luncheon at Buck's has been exploded by Christoby's public ownership, projected profit targets and the arrival of gimlet-eyed men with jutting, Thatcherite jaws rather than the well-bred cutaway chin. Such is the supermarket status of the art houses, Fothers now wonders whether he is any better than a check-out girl or a Volvo dealer from Harlesden. It came as a relief when, without the requisite number of appearances on the *Antiques Roadshow* to justify him, he was rusticated to the country as Christoby's expert in Squireshire and – *sans* Buck's – now has to purvey that wit and charm over lunches at the White Hart.

The Fashion Model

Lily telephones her uncle, the Duke of Portarlington, to ask if she can bring Fernando to do a shoot at Castle Sleight. The Duke is mightily puzzled, since nothing is in season and does his sister know that Lily is hanging around with some damned foreigner. 'He photographed the Super-bra campaign, Uncle Bertie,' she explains and arrives, her emaciated frame shrouded in a designer donkey jacket, accompanied by Fernando and four androgynous assistants. One advantage of Lily's upbringing in large, unheated houses is that she is impervious to cold and can stand for hours in the Armoury, posing against broadswords, wearing little but a cropped top constructed from ten wispy strands of alpaca and costing £785. Despite her chiselled frailty and luminous pallor, Lily is more robust at walking the dogs around the lake at Sleight than drinking Diet Coke in smoke-filled clubs on the models' Milan–Paris–New York circuit. It has been a life of hectic loneliness ever since the Whirlwind model agency plucked her from the sixth form and Lily had to do her A-level revision during casting sessions. The others moan about London Fashion Week, but she is secretly thrilled to be staying with her mother in Cadogan Square, eating M & S crispy aromatic duck in front of the telly. After the transient glamour of the *Vogue* covers and the world's catwalks, her merchant banker will come and Lily will revert to a Georgian house, pearls, three children and tireless campaigning on green issues.

The Bride's Mother

The worst has happened. Just three weeks to go before the wedding, Canon Anstruther has fallen and broken his hip at the church wine and cheese party, is now *hors de combat* in St Michael's Hospital, and Cynthia Montmorency has been told that the locum vicar is a woman. Never in the history of the Montmorencys (many of whom fought at Crécy) has there been an equivalent disaster. As darling Chloë walks up the aisle on her father's arm, her ancestors will be spinning on their tombs in the side chapel. Darling Chloë seems divinely unconcerned; wafting about in the inviolate haze of love, her only practical contribution to the wedding has been to have a new bra fitted at Rigby & Peller. Having decided at the age of seven that she wanted white roses, twenty yards of tulle, ten bridesmaids and 'Glorious Things of Thee are Spoken', she has been entirely happy to leave the details to her mother. Mrs Montmorency is consequently a shredded biscuit. There was the drama with the flowers (roses have to be imported from Holland in April), the unpleasant realisation that the caterers – so stoutly recommended by the bridegroom's mother – could achieve nothing more sophisticated than the asparagus roll, and a grisly moment when the organist came to tea to discuss the niceties of 'God Be in My Head' and the cat was sick on her coat. Other than declaring that no reception for which he is paying will take place in a marquee with a ruched apricot lining, Mr Montmorency has been no help at all; Nanny has said – with an ominous sniff – that the twenty yards of tulle is surely inflammable ('Does Mama want Chloë going up like a torch?'); and the diamonds in the tiara are grubby. In addition to all these grievances, Mrs Montmorency is a woman yet to choose her hat.

The Trainer

Harry is looking forward to Aintree. He has a number of promising runners and is adept at pouring drinks down the owners, although he sometimes wonders if they recognise their own horses. But he sees it as part of his job, like a prep school headmaster, to persuade them that it is worth keeping the boy on at school despite the horrendous bills. The easy charm of the trainer comes from a lifetime in the Lambourn–Marlborough axis, trading wives, stories and horses within the racing fraternity. His father had the stables before him and Harry used to ride, although keeping his damned weight to ten stone involved the nightmare of 'wasting'. He and some of the other jockeys would sweat it out at the Turkish baths in Jermyn Street; as a last resort he'd take pee pills after riding out – you could lose three or four pounds that way but had to stop and nip behind hedges all the way to the races. 'Nowadays the jockeys all have sports psychologists,' he tells the owners. 'But in my day we had a nip of Guinness before a race and a lot more fun.' Harry is an easy raconteur and the owners' wives are pink with pleasure to think that he knows the Princess Royal and has trained for the Queen Mother. Clutching large whiskies in the fuggy bar, they listen avidly to the story of his spectacular crash at Becher's on Bob's My Uncle. *Louche*, relaxed, he includes them on the inside of a glamorous world and never lets on that it was touch and go whether their bloody cart-horses could even run in the Grand National.

The Ethnic Jewellery Designer

The idea for doing marvellous things with beads came to Ellen while on safari in Kenya: the Masai were so inspiring and she returned laden with orangy-brown, misshapen artefacts. Before her girlfriends could say 'Earl's Court Jewellery Fair' Ellen had woven and strung fantastical ropes of seed pods, beaten silver and amusing lumps of driftwood, not to mention the shells acquired during her Christmas holiday in the Caribbean. She started designing on the kitchen table of the capacious house in Camden, making the 'family room' such a regular little hive of industry that her husband, a television executive in a symbiotic relationship with his Psion organiser, had to pick his way to supper over rush baskets full of sharks' teeth. Ellen has been much praised by the *Guardian*'s fashion pages for her inventive ways with dead bits of the natural world. A local authority course on silversmithing has added the bashed saucepan lid dimension to her work, as demonstrated by her earrings and pendant, threaded on a leather thong. 'We have so much to learn from the Asmat tribes,' she says, having read an article on Indonesia in *Marie Claire* and cut out the pictures of the natives in full regalia. Ellen is particularly struck by their use of red since she considers Western society woefully timid about colour, and is currently working with vibrant Venetian glass trading beads acquired in a market in Zanzibar. Her daughter recently came home positively manacled with friendship bracelets: Ellen is considering doing them in silver for her next collection.

The Wine Buff

The Brigadier is a claret man. Fellow guests at the tasting given by wine merchants Gargle & Swill have been reduced to a catatonic trance by his pronouncements that 'the 94s will never come round' and – a death knell delivered with incredulous eyebrow twitching – that he 'cannot get any complexity'. He is much given to the teeth-sucking and expectorating method of tasting, while raising eyes heavenwards in a theatrical performance intended to be noticed. The grand finale is his incredulous surprise that 'they even declared the vintage'. Swirling the wine in his glass, an action punctuated with vacuum-suction sniffing, he name-drops Château Petrus and Romanee Conti, yet at home offers lesser New World wines to impoverished friends who are perfectly capable of going to Oddbins for themselves. Arch little anecdotes about swanky growers are his idea of conversation ('As my friend Christian was saying to me at a lunch in Reims only the other day . . .'). In truth, the Brigadier is not a clubbable man. His days in the regiment are over and total immersion in *Decanter* magazine is not the stuff of repartee, especially when compounded by his bony fingers, extraordinarily wincy little feet for such a florid fellow and the disapproving demeanour. His wispy, sandy-haired wife has long since taken to gardening and whisky as small gestures against being bored into submission. The Brigadier hasn't noticed: his love affair with wine and food has long since replaced his feelings for women.

The Dowager Gardening Expert

Plants stand to attention when they see Hermione coming, so as not to be rootled at by her sticks. Decidedly one of nature's dowager duchesses, complete with diamonds and very good, sensible shoes, she is obsessively discriminating; marigolds and lobelia are her horticultural equivalent of 'toilet' and 'pardon'; let no one even mention the hanging basket and yew is definitely non-yew. She particularly despises anyone who tells her that they've 'got a lovely show' which inevitably means an eyesore in purple, orange and pink. Even the innocent cabbage, once so charming mixed with roses in the old walled vegetable garden, is now highly suspect since some prisoners designed a cabbage display for Chelsea Flower Show. Hermione's expertise lies in arcane grasses and the beneficial habits of the earthworm (soil aeration being so vital). Her idea of annuals is vastly expensive packets of wildflower seeds which need to be scattered over at least four acres for several years running in order to establish a really satisfactory meadow. Her house – a hugger-mugger of good but sadly unpolished furniture, and petrol station glasses thrust into cupboards with Georgian goblets – is in direct variance to the ordered beauty outside. The garden door is propped open with something that is probably a Bernini bust. Snobbery may be in her bones but Hermione is untouched by vanity: her crusted, yellow fingernails are reptilian, peaty deposits have transformed her diamond rings into the rocks of ages and the low-flying bosom is the result of years bent over recalcitrant borders. Amidst the rambly, silvery-white loveliness that is her herbaceous border dwells one startling aberration: the blood-red dahlia Arabian Night. Now everybody wants one.

The Ageing Hippy

Christian is looking forward to taking his two daughters to the Reading Festival – a showy act of parenting, since he was absent from their childhood finding himself on an ashram in India. The girls think he's rather cool, even if he does play 'Lay Lady Lay' agonisingly slowly on the guitar. Christian (he used to be Christopher but found that insufficiently New Age) thinks he's really cool: he's been at the rock-face of cool ever since he read PPE at Oxford and wrote his dissertation to the sound of Captain Beefheart and Cream. His only regret is that he never really knew Howard Marks. Christian's contemporaries embraced Thatcherism, but he remained in a time warp of joss-sticks and ganja; he did set up a mobile pizza business, but the oven broke at Glastonbury so he left it there. Material possessions mean nothing, though he would be mightily inconvenienced if anything interfered with the monthly payments of his private income into a Coutts account. Living in a formalised squat off Ladbroke Grove is mysteriously expensive, though it might be his Knightsbridge doctor's bills – the rare permutation of giardiasis he believes he caught in Kashmir needs constant medical reassurance. He cannot touch meat, only pulses from Portobello Market, to which he travels by bicycle since his Citroen 2CV failed to start one morning. Thus, the girls are going to drive their old man to Reading to hear Black Grape. Hey, one has to stay with it.

The Art Junkie

When Lola is not in an airport she is in an art gallery. She's been to New York for the Howard Hodgkin (she stayed in her apartment on the West Side), to London for the Cézanne (she stayed in her house in the Boltons), to Amsterdam for the Vermeer (she stayed at the Amstel), to Paris for the Dali (she stayed at the Montalembert, so witty since designer Christian Liaigre mixed mediaeval, Roman and art deco with conical steel basins) and now she's nipping back to her villa on Capri for the weekend. But gallery openings are her social ladder, the young men are so attractive, the curators so charming that they make her feel luminously intellectual, and she will be returning for the Froelich Foundation's collaboration with the Tate. 'Darleeng, they will be showing Bruce Nauman – his sculptured neon is *bellissimo!*' Her husband, an elderly patrician banker, prefers Botticelli to Bruce but is entirely happy to indulge Lola's indiscriminate passions for the outrageous, provided he doesn't have to have a formaldehyde badger in any of his drawing-rooms. Her credit card bills are a small price to pay as an insurance policy. And, darleeng, she has seen a leetle Braque – simple blue and white, perfect for the seaside house. Decked in Ungaro, Chanel Rouge Absolu lipstick, Manolo Blahnik shoes and a tiny Kate Spade bag (so wondrously expensive in Bloomingdale's), Lola lauds the purity of minimalism.

The Schoolboy Activist

Roland is a pill. His parents have had to buy four differently coloured dustbins so that tins, paper, bottles and anything remotely biodegradable and stinky can be separated for recycling. He is vegetarian, and his disapproval of red meat, red wine and red-blooded over-indulgence is so palpable that Roland's mother has had to give up Sunday lunch altogether. She is also reduced to puffing Silk Cut after dark in the garden as Roland is a militant anti-smoker. His eco-Stasi reign of terror is equally effective at school where he tells the geography teacher precisely how many trees are being felled per day in the Brazilian rainforest, plus the dire consequences of global warming obliterating East Anglia. It is the what-are-you-going-to-do-about-it tone that grates upon grown-ups, since Roland's freckly fervour can induce guilt about everything from fishing quotas to phosphates. 'Roland is such a little mine of information,' say family friends, dazed by a barrage of facts about the effects of the brutish Japanese appetite for sea cucumbers on the ecology of the Galapagos Islands. He finds it remarkably easy to get sponsorship for charity walks since people will promise any amount of money just to make him go away. His father, whose property deals enabled them to move to a plump Oxfordshire estate, is furious that his hunting is now blighted by Roland's espousal of the whinging, anoraked, unwashed antis. How the hell did he come to have a son who is such a crasher – and, god-dammit, to whom he has to defer?

The Old-fashioned Nanny

Nanny says that a strict routine is best for Baby and when she was with Lady Buxted *her* baby was on a bottle and slept all through the night from the age of three months. Mummy is thus suitably terrified by Nanny as Nanny intends her to be. Nanny says that good children need a lot of fresh air and sets off for Bembridge beach in the teeth of an east wind with Tilly, Orlando and Baby in a Silver Cross pram – trundle, trundle, trundle. Tilly swings on Nanny's hand, crinkly with years of Johnson's baby soap, and wheedles, 'Nanny, can we have bubble gum for tea?' but Nanny says, 'Don't be silly, dear, I've made some nice egg sandwiches.' When Orlando cuts his knee crabbing Nanny kisses it better and says, 'There now,' because she says 'There now' a great deal. Orlando's daddy can remember her saying 'There now' on Bembridge beach in the fifties and is immensely comforted that, in an uncertain world, some things have not changed. 'Do you know, Tilly, Nanny's brother was a stationmaster in Devon, which is where Nanny comes from, and I used to go and stay in their cottage and see all the trains?' Tilly and Orlando are stunned that Nanny comes from anywhere – or has any brothers or sisters – since they imagined she just sprang fully formed into the nursery. Her arms are floury white and strong from picking up Baby and comforting small hurts: 'Diddly-diddly-dee, who's a brave boy then?' Daddy and Orlando secretly agree that the difference between Nanny and Mummy is that when Nanny says 'There now' Mummy would say 'Run along'.

The Hotel Doorman

George has been at the Grand Hotel since the forties. There are customers who say that the day George retires they'll be off to the Inter-Global Glamorama down the road. But George knows they're only joking – they're as traditional as he is, and karaoke evenings at the Glamorama would hold no charms for them. Why, he can remember Lord Freddy Fitznibbins coming to lunch every Sunday with his mother in the early days, rationing having done for their cook. His Lordship still comes, says it's the only place in London where he can get a decent treacle tart. Traditional values, that's what the Grand and George are about. 'Never underestimate tradition,' he tells his grandson Wayne. 'Every prime minister has dined at the Grand since I was a bellboy.' Wayne is more impressed by Liam Gallagher drinking at the Glamorama. George, whose professional gravity has penetrated his home life in Bethnal Green, doesn't know where it will all end. He knows his place, of course, which is above all the other staff in the hotel, but the guests do not seem to know theirs. Some have even summoned their own taxis. That's Germans for you, don't remember who won the war. Still, when Princess Di popped in the other day, she said, 'Hello, George,' (her father was a regular, lovely man) and when he told his wife, Joyce, she'd thought he should write his memoirs. The general manager, a suave cove, suspects George's tips exceed his own salary.

The Weather Girl

Charmian has the requisite blondeness and scintilla of intelligence essential for distracting the viewers from the interminable drizzle, flash floods and those sneaky, pipe-bursting cold snaps that characterise spring. While she is dithering deliciously between camera one and camera two the viewers quite ignore the grim configuration of the isobars on the map behind her. Her perky jacket helps, deliberately chosen to imply sunshine in the teeth of conflicting evidence. Since Charmian's idyll is to sunbathe on the roof terrace of her Chelsea flat, she fails to grasp that farmers need rain, sailors wind and joggers blessedly cool temperatures. The complexity of others' expectations are irrelevant to her overweening ambition to host a television game show and she already has one foot on the sofa of her own breakfast television programme, presenting with cuddly Andy on Fridays. Fame has materialised in fan letters, fashion spreads and feature articles such as 'Me and My Health'. She is, of course, vegetarian (excepting the salmon fishcake at Le Caprice), goes to the gym, doesn't drink (except champagne) and only uses natural cosmetic products that have not been tested on animals (although she hasn't enquired too closely into her Gloss 'n' Go hair spray). Tomorrow may be cloudy with rain at times but for Charmian it will be much brighter later when *OK!* comes to interview her in that sunny little flat.

The Reluctant Debutante

Lucinda, being too fat, too short and too monosyllabic to be the belle of any ball, is only doing the season for her mother. Ever since the last vestiges of Christmas were ruthlessly swept into the dustbin, Mrs Lumley-Smith (who was just Mrs Smith until quite recently) has been planning her Mothers' Lunch. At this high-pitched event a swarm of women with rigid hair will swap little address stickers to put into each others' Filofaxes. Some of them indeed came out themselves in the halcyon days before A-levels made going to Royal Ascot so dreadfully inconvenient. 'I've said to Lucinda that really a typing course and some cookery lessons would stand her in much better stead than silly old exams, but she won't listen,' is a familiar wail. Lucinda secretly thinks that sitting an A-level in Sanskrit would be less terrifying than going to a dance; she is sadly aware that taffeta, frills and bows do not become her, suspecting she looks like a pink blancmange. 'Nonsense, dear,' says her mother, all toothy and keen. July is a maelstrom of drinks parties, fizzing with the happy release from exam trauma and contemplation of a gap year backpacking in Vietnam. Lucinda, to her surprise, finds that she is rather enjoying herself. Anything, indeed, would be better than Cheltenham Ladies' College. Camilla has become her new best friend and Wimbledon is awfully good fun; Lucinda's godmother is a debenture holder and takes her to see Tim Henman. When she joins Camilla's family in Tuscany during August she will actually be quite chatty. By the end of the year, if not exactly a swan, Lucinda will, at least, be less of a goose.

The Fashion Photographer

Tony has seen it all, mate. You can't impress him with pulchritude. Put Claudia Schiffer in front of his lens and he'd say, over a Rolling Rock in the bar at Kartouche, that he had seen prettier traffic wardens. 'Mind you, if you put her hair with Naomi's bum and Elle's legs then you'd really have a supermodel.' The nips and tucks of the entire cast of *Hello!* magazine are his badinage, for the fashion photographer is an encyclopaedia of the defects of the famous. His ambition is to do something radical with an advertising campaign using Jacob sheep – sort of Damien Hirst meets Guess? jeans. Then he will receive the photographic Oscar: a contract with *Harper's Bazaar*, provider of apartments, air fares and the sort of cachet that enables Steven Meisel to eschew vulgarities such as check-in procedures at hotels. Someone else does it for him; hard for Tony to believe as he watches his cheery but hungover assistant arrive late on a motorbike. Meisel is Tony's antichrist, likewise Avedon. Annie Liebovitz? Oh, please. Who needs to go to Sarajevo to prove their cred? (Tony is secretly unnerved by Leibovitz, being himself unable either to book the whole of LA for a shoot or be a lesbian.) As for Herb Ritts, well, love, if you shoot enough rolls you're bound to get a good picture. This violently critical insouciance impresses the animated ironing board on whom he is photographing crushed velvet for *Elle*; likewise the retro-chic of his entirely filthy car, his casual ensemble of black, black and Timberland boots and awesome ability to chew gum, smoke, answer his mobile telephone and have his assistant set up the shot simultaneously. But, of course, Tony would never go out with a model: they're too stupid, mate.

The Lady Writer

Veronica's long-awaited biography of Cecily Savage, the bisexual poet and muse of the Archimedes Group, is confidently expected to win the Rosebery Award. A chain smoker of untipped cigarettes, Veronica enlivens the North London dinner party circuit with throaty anecdotes and is considered madly intellectual because she cuts her own hair. A small inheritance and a large, shabby house on the Hampstead–Highgate borders enable her to give soirées for the *jeunesse* who are no longer *dorée* but rather badly shaven, with brown-stained mouths like old spaniels and the sort of sagging corduroy jackets that make them indistinguishable from Veronica's sofas. All have written worthy and impenetrable books and, over the warm Soave, discourse in high-pitched wails about their publishers' hopeless proofreading, mingy advances and how Martin Amis distorts the market. To a man they approve of literary prizes for women only. 'You should have been a judge of the Tangerine Prize, Veronica,' they say. 'By the by, there isn't any whisky, is there?' Veronica indulges this extended family but reserves uncritical affection for her cats and her garden. Animals and plants have no instinct for her weaknesses, unlike the absurd literary editors.

The Tory Back-bencher

Sir Anthony Blanding is in effulgent mood. He has been lunched well by a lobbyist and can now enjoy a somnolent interlude in the chamber to justify his pre-prandial drink in Annie's Bar. The debate is to be on war widows' pensions, a subject for which Sir Anthony has a sentimental affection since he ostensibly received his knighthood for tireless work on behalf of ex-servicemen and their dependants. In reality the gong was, of course, for some thirty-five years of doing as he was told by the Whips' Office. There was a time during the Macmillan years when he was a bright young PPS, but he never got on with that surly fellow Heath and by the time Margaret came along – damned fine woman, no Euro-dithering from her – Sir Anthony had settled into being a backwoodsman. He is soundly against the single currency and in favour of capital punishment and blood sports. Many a lunch at Brooks's has been spent fulminating about this gun-control nonsense. There is a thriving gun club in his Middle England constituency whose members have been making Sir Anthony's life hell at his Saturday morning surgeries. Now the hullabaloo of the General Election is over, he is settling into a life of decent obscurity, thankful that at least his daughter had her wedding reception on the House of Commons terrace during the glory days. It is all so very different now – the declaration of interests has stymied fact-finding missions to Tuscany and the new boys in the House are workaholic puritans with mobile telephones. Wistfully longing for a farewell peerage, he prays the Lords won't be abolished. Lady Blanding, a fearsomely competent woman with a bridge four, says that he must have somewhere to go during the day.

The Teenage Partygoer

It is absolutely essential that Annabel leaves the house for the Feathers Ball before her father sees what she is wearing. Or rather what she is not wearing. But when caught shovelling a packet of ten Marlboro, a bottle of Anäis Anäis and Clorets chewing gum into a black nylon rucksack, Annabel says, 'Dad, get a life, you're a stiff. You think I should be wearing a smocked dress or something. I'm fifteen, you know.' Dad suddenly realises that he is sharing the house with an alien. 'Your Daughter,' he says with fatal emphasis to his wife, 'has a tattoo.' Annabel's shoulders do the teenage don't-you-know-anything shrug as she explains that the tattoo is washable and doesn't imply she's on drugs. She begs both parents not to humiliate her by collecting her in the family space-wagon and *promises* on her honour to return with her friend Charlotte. Once at the dance she hangs out with other friends from St Mary's in a state of chattering excitement induced by furious smoking and taking two aspirin with Coca-Cola. Will Tom, who she met in Sotogrande during the summer, be there? She thought he was really cool, with his tan and riding a Vespa. He now has the pallor and spots induced by the intervening school term, but when he braves the girlish gaggle to extract her on to the dance floor, he is, as far as she is concerned, Brad Pitt. Annabel allows him to snog her. Returning home, she and Charlotte make piles of toast and Marmite, leaving the kitchen a war zone of crumbs. When Annabel's father asks if they had fun (meaning is Annabel already pregnant?) Annabel shrugs and says, 'Nothing much happened, actually. It was OK, that's all.'

The Weekenders

Tim and Louisa bought Rose Cottage to escape the noisome sophistication of Fulham, eat *salade niçoise* off Peter Jones teak furniture in the garden and finally find the time to read Michael Ondaatje. A year later they have discovered that the lawn does not mow itself, the windows are wonky – admitting a sinuous draft on the forty-eight weekends when there is no sunshine – and *salade niçoise* is an impossibility since there are no anchovies in the country. The village shop in Little Wapshott sells only white sliced bread and tinned sweetcorn. They now bring all their food down from London, ditto plants since the local garden centre is quite five miles away; loading the car on a Friday night is an exhausting prelude to the two-hour drive and arrival in a chill darkness alleviated only by a note from Mrs Blodgett (who had seemed such a treasure) saying they've run out of fire-lighters. Louisa is bewildered by always having her clothes in the wrong house, and is beginning to think that Wellington green is her least favourite colour, but for just twenty-five minutes prior to lunch on Sunday, when they've got the heating working, the fire lit and stopped feeling simply furious, it is all worth it. Then they have to pack up the car, including the little pieces of cheese they can't bear 'to go to waste', and return to London in a steaming traffic jam. Neither Tim nor Louisa has even opened *The English Patient*.

The Vet

Clive is the lodestar of every sensitive soul racked with worry about the delicate constitution of their West Highland terrier, Pekingese or arthritic Dachshund. His rugged charm is a consistent reassurance about the perils of discs slipped on London's treacherous pavements and the advisability of teeth scaling. 'Naughty plaque, Tulip. You must get her to eat more bikkie, Lady Amanda,' he says with fatherly concern. Lady Amanda is quite besotted. When Tulip had puppies Clive actually made a home visit to mother and babies and inspected all the male puppies with the words: 'And are we a proper little gentleman?' His surgery has a heart-wrenching pin board covered with snapshots of liquid-eyed patients and a petition for Passports for Pets. Tins of Hill's Science Diet are displayed enticingly on the shelves since obesity is sadly prevalent in Chelsea and Belgravia. As Clive prepares to cut Tulip's nails, he ruefully observes her consort, Bonbon, heavily settled on the weighing platform. 'Perhaps Bonbon thinks that if he stays there long enough, the scales will go down,' he twinkles. Lady Amanda returns on the smallest pretext, even grass seeds between Tulip's toes. How could she resist a man who says 'Bless you' to a dog when it sneezes?

The Fashion Eccentric

A *mélange* of Christian Lacroix, the thrift shop and her grandmother's evening bag distinguishes Nancy's toilette. The effect is that of a one-woman party stopper. She has no idea, nor would care, that she looks like Madonna crossed with the Mad Hatter. Her face – little eyes bemused with short sight, scarlet lipstick smudged from application in the taxi – bears scant relation to her finery. Clothes to her are beautiful objects. She would shudder to think that they had anything to do with fashion. Nancy has an entire cupboard devoted to hats, none of which has been anywhere near such a vulgar occasion as Ascot. Some she uses as interior decoration – a charming purple fez adorns a bust of Caesar in her library. Many have cheered the book launches that are part of her social whirl as a writer of pithy reviews for small-circulation magazines. Deep in inscrutable biographies, the fashion eccentric has no time for shopping – too common and unimaginative. She acquires clothes in junk shops, markets, at auction. A crocodile Kelly bag was a triumph of bidding at Christie's ten years ago. The modern equivalent, so easily available in Bond Street, would mean nothing to her. A sadness has been the disappearance of good twenties clothes from the Lanes in Brighton; Nancy cherishes trailing scarves bought there years ago on a student budget. She has always had an eye, relishing combinations of texture and colour bewildering to her friends, and secretly hoping that the peacock finery distracts attention from her big feet.

The Bird-watcher

A slight trembling of her binoculars betrays Hester's delight at having spotted the willow warbler. That she knows it to be a willow warbler, rather than a reed warbler, is a measure of her expertise in LBJs – the ornithological term for Little Brown Jobs. Any fool with the *Observer Book of Birds* can identify an avocet in Norfolk, but it takes real LBJ discrimination to tell a skylark from a shore lark. Hester is one such purist. Not for her the vulgar activities of the twitchers, a rogue species of bird enthusiast who cannot detect the chirr of a nightjar but clock up sightings of rare species via fast cars, mobile telephones and e-mail. No sooner has a Siberian finch landed in a suburban garden than the twitchers are there with long lenses. Hester disdains such sensationalism and has devoted herself to the habits of the little ringed plover. Others might dream of going to the Galapagos to see the blue-footed booby, but Hester's idea of bliss is St Kilda via a converted herring trawler to study the web-footed wren. She also has a decided weakness for puffins. In the great binoculars-versus-telescopes debate, Hester is a bins not a 'scope girl. Her only remotely twitcherish vice is spotting the birds seen on television; nature programmes don't count, but the coverage of the Falklands war provided some splendid sightings. She is currently collecting twelve volumes on the Palaearctic birds and in March will give a little talk on Our Migratory Friends in aid of the church spire.

The Hiker

Harold the hiker knows more about the countryside than anyone who actually lives in it; he feels passionately about rights of way and the concept of any private ownership within a national park is an affront to his civil liberties. The results of this mind-set are potentially explosive as Mr Twemlow, scion of eight generations of Twemlows to have farmed in the Peak District, considers Harold to be a miserable little bugger with a left-wing beard and a degree in pathological stupidity from Manchester-bloody-University. The very sight of a piece of Polartec and a bedroll gives Twemlow teeth-grinding anxiety about open gates and miscarrying sheep. Harold would be similarly apoplectic to think his country code of practice could ever be called into question. He lives in Didsbury, a misfortune necessitated by working in adult education, but every weekend chugs towards Glossop and High Peak in his trusty second-hand Volvo. He has added to the erosion of the Pennine Way, re-enacted the mass trespass on Kinder Scout and regards Mam Tor as salutary training for his holiday assaults on the Munroes. A man who studies Ordnance Survey maps in the minute detail others devote to nuclear fission, Harold has had many a merry hour over a pint of Fiddler's Elbow discussing the exact number of Munroes – Scottish hills over 3,000 feet – with fellow hirsute enthusiasts. He himself is a 311 man, although there are persuasive arguments for 319, it all depends on how you measure the contours. When there were but 295 Munroes an awesome fellow called Hamish McWhatsit climbed the lot in 100 days – the very thought makes Harold's eyes revolve excitedly behind his glasses. Setting out to emulate this feat, loins girded with Gore-tex, Harold is exactly the sort of amateur dreaded by the mountain rescue services.

The Weight Watcher

Once Lizzie used to wear Biba in size eight, a memory tragically at variance with the collapsed shopping bag that is now her body. Was it three children, two decades of bad dinner parties or the innumerable glasses of white wine that did it? Whatever – the time has come for a Last Stand. When a woman starts cutting the size 16 labels out of her Marks & Spencer's skirts a Rubicon is crossed: she realises that it is no longer enough to have thin ankles. Lizzie has now tried the Scarsdale Diet, the Hay Diet and the Nigel Lawson Diet without enthusiasm or success. She would dearly love to toss her meagre allowance of calories over the windmill of the Dine Out and Lose Weight Diet but chance would be a fine thing. Her husband's idea of eating out is Wheeler's at lunch-time. The prospect of Weightwatchers looms and Lizzie has a recurring nightmare of standing up in a chill Clapham church hall saying, 'I am Lizzie and I weigh eleven and a half stone.' She realises that exercise is the only answer but is utterly daunted by Lycra shorts and falling over in an aerobics class. Lizzie once shared a personal trainer with Ginny and Ruth who live in the same street; they moved the sofas to one side in the knock-through sitting-room and grunted on the fitted carpet. It was so depressing she had several enormous glasses of M & S Orvieto, then pasta at lunch the next day to absorb the hangover. But her diet is *definitely* starting tomorrow.

The Femme Fatale

The mysterious allure of the *femme fatale* has very little to do with sex appeal. She has it, of course, but as an inherent quality, not the artificial veneer of streaked blonde, Versace-clad pretenders. Kate has style, not designer labels, which usually means she dresses in black with rather good jewellery: Miriam Haskell pieces acquired long before paste became fashionable, or the silver and gold *bonbouches* from Kiki McDonough that are consistently laid at her shrine. It is the lack of the obvious that constitutes her *fatale* attraction. She is entirely comfortable wherever she is, whoever she is with, which gives her companions a sense of sunny warmth. She knows how to do everything so well that other women are in awe of her. That she is frighteningly well read and rather clever is offset by wit and depth of character: men are spellbound by her ability to listen, women flattered that she should accept invitations to their parties, if secretly daunted. No one quite knows what she does – the title editor-at-large is a cosmopolitan conundrum – but it takes her smoothly to Long Island, Bali, Los Angeles and Patmos. Her time and money seem admirably under her own control and when in London she can be found not in an office but in a small, pretty flat on Chelsea Embankment to which an enslaved decorator friend has done fantastically clever things with halogen lighting. There are always fresh flowers. Men would do anything for her – the elusive *femme fatale*'s appeal is that she does not seem to need them.

The History Don

Richard is demented with anxiety. The profitable pursuits of book reviewing and media punditry ('Whither the British constitution by 2000?') are about to be interrupted by the new term. And, even more tiresome, new students. The boys will wear earrings after a gap year teaching Nepalese children and the girls will be imagining that they are Zuleika Dobson. The girls are more distracting, their hero-worship being touchingly transparent. They have, of course, seen him on television. 'Richard Norman is the regius professor of modern history at Balniel College. Professor, how are we to account for this latest resurgence of neo-fascism in Germany?' 'Well, Jeremy, to analyse the pugnacious German national character I feel we really have to go back to the time of Frederick Barbarossa . . .' In his rooms all flat surfaces are so suffocated by academic detritus that he conducts most winter tutorials in the pub. His house (Victorian, rolling lawn, somnolent stream) and even his Morris Minor overflow with books in ragged piles, annotated with yellowing A4 notes to which he rarely refers. His career as the rent-a-woolly-jumper historian is inspired by spontaneous erudition; that is what Camille — twenty-one, loose-limbed, sleepy-eyed and gorgeously intelligent — loved about him. Richard wonders if his macrobiotic wife Frances, an English graduate who breast-fed four children and is now immersed in a dissertation on Anglo-Saxon place names, ever noticed the affair or chose to ignore it. Camille writes sometimes; maybe a new muse will emerge this autumn.

The Museum Attendant

Kathleen has a bovine immobility that makes the patience of Job seem inconsequential. For fifteen years she has sat on a plastic chair in the antiquities department of the Bolingbroke Museum, guardian of the national collection of Iron Age arrowheads. It is significantly quiet in this section but Kathleen nevertheless exercises eternal vigilance, ever on the alert for smokers and closet sandwich-eaters amongst the rare, mild-mannered arrowhead enthusiasts who find their way through from the racier exhibits. She secretly yearns to be moved to mummies, to be caught up in the hectic whirl of school groups doing projects on the pyramids, but her superintendent says, 'Oh no, it takes someone of experience to be in Iron Age, Kathleen,' and so she remains, returning each evening to her cats in Croydon to jot a hopelessly romantic novel about trysts among the pottery shards. The protagonists bear absolutely no relation to the spotty individuals in anoraks, woolly socks and sandals who frequent antiquities. Nor do Kathleen's wildest imaginings embrace the trendy new curator's plans for a touchy-feely interactive 'Iron Age Experience' funded by the National Lottery. She dreams that one day a BBC documentary team will come, that her deep knowledge of archaeology will be unearthed by an intuitive researcher, that she will be seen on camera being calmly efficient, answering enquiries with quiet authority. The mundane truth day-to-day is that the question she is most frequently asked is the way to the lavatory.

The Air Stewardess

Cheryl's brittle smile is professionally deceptive. She hates you. Even as the captain is announcing that 'the head of our cabin staff today is Cheryl Fishface, whose pleasure it will be to serve you on our flight to the Costa del Lager' she has identified the man in seat 29B as trouble. He had the impertinence to ask for a newspaper and Cheryl's worked on Plummit Airlines long enough to know that such arcane requests, unless nipped in the bud with a stiff word, can lead to hot towels, eye masks and extra miniatures of Bailey's Irish Cream. Her legs, despite the American Tan support pantihose, are killing her and the baby belonging to the couple from Wolverhampton is grizzling. She wonders, she really does, how anybody can think that being an air hostess is glamorous. Two days' layover in the Lager Beach Jollity Inn is hardly the Carlyle, New York. As she puts on her floral pinny and prepares the in-flight meal Cheryl becomes an airborne prefect: 'Will you be having the chicken or the beef, sir?' she threatens, dispensing the silver-foil trays with a pair of tongs. It is her considered opinion that the four lads in smoking should have an extremely limited amount of alcoholic refreshment. 'Now, young men,' she says. 'We don't want to have to pour you off the plane, do we?' It is Plummit's policy to endorse the motherly approach to the talking parcels, as the punters are known. Cheryl is hoping her rigid charms will upgrade her to First Class duties on the Far Eastern routes, a nirvana of wealthy businessmen too exhausted to eat or drink. The sobriquet 'trolley dolly' is not one which could ever be applied to her.

The Life Peeress

Baroness Escrick of Easingwold is a trooper successively drilled on the front lines of the parish council, the district council, the county council and assorted working parties on juvenile delinquency and family values. Wherever two people are gathered together, Isabel Escrick can chair a committee. Once a land-girl, now a sound advocate for a return to the three Rs, school uniform and parental responsibility, she is regarded as a safe pair of hands. Striding through the lobbies with the same vigour she applied to the Yorkshire moors as a girl, Lady Escrick's good sense can be relied upon for everything from under-age sex to lavatories for the disabled. She is a popular contributor to *Any Questions* (the sort who receives solid audience support when the programme comes from a spa town), chancellor of a provincial university and a rather jolly grandmother. Her husband has died long since, exhausted by his wife's exhortation never to underestimate what he could achieve in ten minutes, and Lady Escrick now descends upon their children – reputable lawyers and accountants all – and is surprisingly adept at playing Cluedo and making bread sauce. She then trundles off in her Rover (one must always buy British), back to the stout mansion block in Kensington where her companions are malt whisky and a vigorous amount of paperwork. Knowing everyone, asked everywhere, Isabel Escrick has the inestimable grace never to stay long. After all, she is a very busy woman.

The Minimalist Architect

Richard Richenbeck has reduced minimalism to nothingness, a feat proportionally inverse to his fee. The tyranny with which he has suppressed the decorative instincts of the rich and famous to one single white orchid is legendary. Then there was the absurdly fashionable couple to whom he denied a coat cupboard lest it should spoil the line of the hall. Upon entering their exquisite house they are now perpetually condemned to seeing the nanny's Drizabone plonked on the one Biedermeier chair. Carrara marble, stainless steel, etched glass and the sort of superwaif staircases that undulate upward like serpents are the signatures for which clients fly him round the world. Richenbeck doesn't care for the country unless it is another country; once, when asked to redesign some stables he asked if the horses were absolutely necessary. The shops he has breathed upon are white vacuums, save for one folded lilac shirt in a perspex case. His restaurants are quintessentially chrome, with all the architectural ingredients on the outside, and the result is curiously Stansted Airport. The Zen purity of his designs is such that Mrs Richenbeck is gamely struggling in a kitchen without knobs, and all the period details that make other houses in Little Venice so charming have been expunged to create one aching void of neutrality in which all the fireplaces are halfway up the wall. The words 'Aga', 'family portraits' and 'Granny's collection of Meissen' are anathema to Richenbeck's soul.

The Shampooist

Michelle has developed a unique form of interrogative English. 'Are you going out tonight?' is her *pièce de resistance*, delivered in an accent that could open a tin, while she dabs ineffectually at the head wrenched over the basin in front of her. Seasonal variations include 'It's ever so cold/warm, isn't it?' and 'Going anywhere nice on your holidays, then?' – both precursors to 'Will you be having the conditioner?' A mere £1 tip cannot be expected to induce a soliloquy on antidisestablishmentarianism. On the train home to Surbiton, Michelle dreams of the day she will have her own salon (called the Cutting Edge) and lucrative range of aromatherapy shampoos for problem hair. Intensive clubbing will punctuate the several years at college doing hairdressing studies which stand between her and being Nicky Clarke. Indeed, her mum sometimes says, 'Really, Michelle, I don't know how you get up in the morning, I really don't – you're not taking any of those nasty tablets, are you?' Michelle's vices actually consist of Red Bull, Silk Cut and chips, thus she is ever so sympathetic to the trials of greasy hair. 'It's dreadful being in a smoky room, Mrs Mortimer, it really makes one's hair smell, doesn't it?' she says sympathetically while yanking a comb through tangled streaks. 'Would you like a tea or coffee? Milk and sugar?' Sometimes, when cutting up little strips of foil for the highlights, she wonders if it is all worth it. Her boyfriend, a personal trainer, says they should think about setting up their own leisure centre – aerobics, beauty, a boutique and a nice juice bar. And Michelle, stuffing the damp towels into the washing machine, thinks, 'Why not?'

The Office Partygoers

Kevin in computer systems has long wanted to discuss his integrated communications packages with Susie in sales. Now, emboldened by warm white wine, he props himself conversationally against her filing cabinet. This manoeuvre does not escape the notice of Miss Bodkin, the chairman's secretary and self-appointed sex policeman of the office party. There will be no bad behaviour at Grinde & Grimlett as long as Miss Bodkin can insert herself between seasonal conviviality under the pretext of proffering the crisps. She has always rather approved of Kevin – such a nice young man in his blazer and golf club tie – and is sorely disappointed to see him succumb to the flagrant attractions of Susie's sweater. Susie, having frequently refilled her paper cup with Cockatoo Ridge Chardonnay, is now talking with confidence – despite gargling the longer words – about strategic contributions. Behind her, unnatural sounds are emanating from the photocopying room. Miss Bodkin is hideously torn between investigating these and rescuing the chairman from the beery imprecations of Ron from the mail room. And over in the far corner, the chairman's wife has backed into the office rubber plant in a desperate attempt to escape from Trevor in diversification. Trevor's theory about how-we-at-Grinde-&-Grimlett-are-rationalising-our-Euro-strategy is almost too much even for Miss Bodkin to bear but she goes nobly to the rescue. The carpet is now crunchy with broken crisps. Tomorrow she'll hoover and tut-tut over the cigarette ends in strange places before shopping for the Christmas she will spend alone with her cat.

The Young Guards Officer

Charlie could have bought his life off the peg at Gieves & Hawkes, complete with the black labrador and the black Volkswagen Golf. He went into the Life Guards after a grisly spell at a crammer resitting the A-levels he flunked at Harrow but, should he ever be posted anywhere, there will be a sound like ripping Elastoplast as he is parted from the King's Road. Charlie was brought up in Chelsea by a doting mother with a spindly house in Markham Square; he has now migrated with the great herd of the middle class to Fulham but it's the bit that's nearly Chelsea and he can walk to La Famiglia. Everything in his red-brick house with its double-fronted sitting-room is pretending to be Wiltshire: the club fender, his late father's military memorabilia, the Thorburn prints of bemused pheasants. Charlie's girlfriend, Lucinda, made the Colefax & Fowler curtains and they bought all the Emma Bridgewater mugs in the General Trading Company. Lucinda and the labrador, equally smitten by Charlie's easy charm and comforting inability to do anything unpredictable, regard him with uncritical affection. He also looks splendid in uniform and on a horse. These virtues, together with scrupulous good manners, will ensure a pleasantly unspectacular army career, a jocund popularity with his brother officers and a steady stream of shooting invitations. When he leaves the regiment he will become an estate agent.

The Shooting Wife

Mrs Pemberton has weathered in the heather. She is never happier than when standing by her man on the moor discussing the challenging volatility of the grouse, wind and rain being nothing a hot bath and a stout whisky won't sort out later. Upholstered in hairy green garments and an ancient hat, she joins the keepers during pheasant shooting convinced that her Sandringham-bred labrador, Jorrocks, is invaluable at picking up. Actually, it dashes madly along the line deaf to a piercing whistle equally marketable as a rape alarm. Eleanor Pemberton is expert at wringing injured birds by the neck and producing steak and kidney pie – the staple of her shooting lunches. 'Nothing like it for the chaps,' she barks through a mouthful of gristle. Dinner will be brown lumps of birds prized from the permafrost of her deep freeze: the words 'vegetarian' and 'anti-blood sports' are ones about which she stands no nonsense. And perhaps you wouldn't mind moving away from the one smouldering log in the fire so Jorrocks can get dry?

The Plumber

The pipes have burst, the heating has imploded with a seismic rumble and there is no hot water. Enter Terry. To those blessed with fecund radiators he might seem a dodgy yob with a gross haircut and a beer belly but to Mrs Bingham his appearance is equivalent only to the Second Coming. Her domestic life is in his hands, a fact of which Terry is thoroughly aware as she fusses around making him tea with three sugars. After one authoritative glance at the boiler he sucks a considered breath through his teeth and opines, more in sorrow than in anger, 'It's the thermostat, missis. And I dunno what cowboy did yer plumbing for yer but it's a new heater, I'm afraid. Oh dear, oh dear.' A beatific smile then accompanies the good news: 'Still, missis, a Fabwarm – top of the range – is only £750 and I might be able to fit it on Thursday.' It is at this point that Mrs Bingham's spine stiffens. She dignifies Terry with the sort of crisp retort normally reserved for recalcitrant sales girls in Peter Jones and, feeling himself reduced to the 'little man' status, Terry dives back into the boiler room waving a spanner. Twenty minutes later he emerges triumphant, quite unable to believe Mrs B's luck as by an extraordinary chance he, Terry, had just the right copper widget to see her right. 'Nothing to it, missis, that'll just be £50 for my call-out fee and £7.80 for parts. A pleasure to do business with you.'

The New Year's Eve Party

Humphrey and Amelia consider that there is nothing happy about the New Year. Humphrey has, perforce, to give up drink since his liver has run up a white flag. Amelia is smoking stoically through the last forty before midnight. Their income tax is due on Tuesday, their pipes have frozen and out in the ether of misery that is January looms an impertinent visit from English Heritage. And so they have come to celebrate at the Anstruthers', as they do every New Year's Eve. It is a purgatorial party held in Nigel Anstruther's billiard room, heated by a dismal coal grate. Festive decoration is limited to a party popper that got stuck in the stag's antlers last year. Nigel is notoriously frugal with the booze: 'Bloody man's got barbed wire around his wallet,' mutters Humphrey as he nurses the supermarket own-brand Scotch. Amelia sorrowfully waves away the screw-top two-litre bottle of red wine. Not even taking Panadol before going to bed would be sufficient to counteract its virulence. There is little food, as everyone has been at rather merry dinner parties which they have left reluctantly. 'Darling, do you absolutely promise you won't accept Flappy and Nigel's invitation next year? Wouldn't it be marvellous just to stay at home?' But of course they never would. It is traditional to abandon a nice warm house to drive twenty miles along icy lanes to a God-awful party at which the host confuses his old sixties records with entertainment. The maudlin merriment is exacerbated by fear: was the old year really so bad after all? The future never seems less inviting than when hyped with 'Auld Lang Syne' and Flappy Anstruther's kedgeree.

The Spinster Aunt

(on front jacket)

Aunt Rosamund is coming to stay for Christmas. So is her dog, Pickle, whose intentions towards the tree are entirely dishonourable. While all around her swab the carpet with Perrier water and kitchen towel, Aunt Rosamund remains sublimely unmoved. Such equilibrium is achieved by living alone and the independence of a private income. There was a romance, long ago, with the son of a Methodist minister but he died of pneumonia, an act for which Rosamund (who's never had a day's ill health) has not quite forgiven him. Gin, bridge, cigarettes and a certain amount of spirited foreign travel have since replaced the unreliability of men. She was one of the first to go fishing for the mighty *mahseer* in Nepal and has lived in an elephant camp in Botswana. The children are riveted by Auntie Rosamund's traveller's tales ('Tell us about the cobra again!') and the Christmas presents garnered in outlandish markets. Her stern exterior belies an inexhaustible enthusiasm for Racing Demon, charades and astringent gossip. Even her nephew-in-law concedes that Auntie is a pretty good egg, despite the bloody dog. Rosamund may drop fag ash on the bedclothes but she never arrives without bringing a case of good champagne.